DINOSA

Anna Pomaska

DOVER PUBLICATIONS, INC.
Mineola, New York

Bibliographical Note

Dinosaurs is a new work, first published by Dover Publications, Inc., in 1998.

International Standard Book Number: 0-486-40162-6

Manufactured in the United States of America
Dover Publications, Inc., 31 East 2nd Street, Mineola, N.Y. 11501

TYRANNOSAURUS (tie-RAN-oh-SAW-rus)

This was one of the biggest meat-eating dinosaurs of all time. It had very big, sharp teeth so it could hunt and kill other dinosaurs.

TRICERATOPS (try-SER-a-tops)

When you count the horns on this dinosaur, you will see why its name means "three-horned face."

Here is a Triceratops mother and baby. These dinosaurs, when grown up, were as big as elephants and liked to travel in large herds.

The hungry Tyrannosaurus is thinking he will make a meal of the peaceful plant-eating Triceratops.

Triceratops does not like to fight, but she can protect herself. She will use her three sharp horns if she needs to.

ELASMOSAURUS (ee-LAZ-moe-SAW-rus)

Elasmosaurus was a giant sea reptile that had a very long neck. It used its neck to catch fish for dinner.

STEGOSAURUS (STEG-oh-SAW-rus)

This dinosaur had large bony plates sticking up out of its back. It had four long spikes on the end of its tail to protect itself.

CAMARASAURUS (kam-AR-a-SAW-rus)

Camarasaurus was a gentle giant. He was
big, heavy, slow-moving, and ate only plants.

ARCHAEOPTERYX (ark-ee-OP-ter-ix)

Archaeopteryx looked like a little dinosaur
with wings. It had feathers and is
the first known bird.

ANKYLOSAURUS (an-KY-low-SAW-rus)

This dinosaur only ate plants, but it had an armor of bone and horns and a tail club that it used to protect itself.

DEINONYCHUS (DIE-no-NIKE-us)

The name of this dinosaur means "terrible claw." He had a big claw shaped like a curved sword on each of his feet.

APATOSAURUS (a-PAT-oh-SAW-rus)

This dinosaur was once called "Brontosaurus" because its bones were discovered by two different scientists who thought they had discovered two different dinosaurs.

Apatosaurus was a very heavy and tall
dinosaur that ate only plants (but lots
and lots of them!).

ICHTHYOSAURUS (ICK-thee-oh-SAW-rus)

Ichthyosaurus was an ocean reptile that had fins and flippers instead of legs. It looked and swam like dolphins of today.

PSITTACOSAURUS (si-TAK-oh-SAW-rus)

Psittacosaurus had a beak which made
this dinosaur look like a parrot.

PARASAUROLOPHUS (par-a-SAWR-oh-LOAF-us)

This was one of the duck-billed dinosaurs that made loud sounds through the long tube on top of its head.

CORYTHOSAURUS (ko-RITH-oh-SAW-rus)

This was another duck-billed dinosaur that made a loud noise through a fan-shaped crest on top of its head.

PTERANODON (tair-AN-oh-don)

Pteranodon was a reptile with very long wings. He could glide on the air and swoop down to catch a fish dinner from the sea.

IGUANODON (i-GWA-no-DON)

Iguanodon had a big spike for a thumb
which helped protect him.

OVIRAPTOR (OVE-ih-RAP-tor)

Oviraptor found other dinosaurs' nests
and stole eggs from them. He broke open
the eggs with his big beak and ate them.

SPINOSAURUS (SPINE-o-SAW-rus)

This strange dinosaur had a huge sail along its back.

BAROSAURUS (BAR-oh-SAW-rus)

Barosaurus was a giant dinosaur that had
a very long neck and tail. Sometimes
a Barosaurus would live to be 100 years old!

A baby Barosaurus stayed close to his mother
for protection until he grew up. Then he would
be so huge he would weigh more than
8 elephants put together!

23

PROTOCERATOPS (pro-toe-SER-a-tops)

Protoceratops laid many eggs in nests made of sand. Her little babies hatched by cracking open the shells and climbing out.

STRUTHIOMIMUS (STROOTH-ee-oh-MIME-us)

Struthiomimus means "ostrich mimic" and this dinosaur acted and looked very much like a big bird without feathers.

PACHYCEPHALOSAURUS
(PAK-ee-CEF-al-oh-SAW-rus)

These dinosaurs had hard bony heads that looked like crash helmets.

They used their heads in butting contests to see who was stronger. The two in this picture are about to bump into each other right now!

STYRACOSAURUS (sty-RAK-oh-SAW-rus)

Styracosaurus looked very scary with all of his horns and spikes, but he only liked to eat plants.

LAMBEOSAURUS (LAM-bee-oh-SAW-rus)

Lambeosaurus has come down to the river
for a drink of water. Like Styracosaurus,
she only eats plants.

MAIASAURA (MY-a-SAW-ra)

Maiasaura was a good mother. She stayed
with her children and brought them leaves
to eat until they grew old enough
to take care of themselves.